SIMPLE HABITS OF
EXTRAORDINARY
SALESPEOPLE

MICHAEL **HANNON**

Dedication

I was very fortunate to begin my career as a salesperson with a great mentor, Mr. Charles Johnson. He provided encouragement and disciplined guidance teaching me the habits of an accomplished salesperson. His lessons were many, but each held an underlying theme: *have the courage to be boldly honest, the skill to outperform expectations, and enjoy enthusiasm for the task that follows.*

His guidance allowed me to enjoy accomplishments far greater than any I had previously imagined.

Several years after I began my career, Mr. Johnson congratulated me on a promotion I received. I thanked him for his guidance and encouragement. I told Charlie Johnson I didn't know how to thank him.

He smiled and said, "I also tried to thank my mentor, Michael. My mentor replied, The only way you can thank me is by finding another you believe has the courage to be boldly honest, will tenaciously pursue outperforming expectations, have enthusiasm for the task and offer them the hand of encouragement."

It is now my turn to pass on the favor of that education.

Acknowledgments

Joshua Stern: The epitome of a high-integrity realtor commented at the conclusion of a presentation, *"Michael, write the book."* Josh's comment became the force that would not allow me to rest until this book was complete. Here it is, Josh.

Kailash Black: I was privileged to find this observant editor, talented book designer, and efficient print-production specialist.

Ervin Dahima: A talented "all-things-digital" specialist who always went above and beyond each task. His wonderful, experienced guidance is always encouraging.

Jose Hernandez: For his artistic talent and especially for this book cover design.

SIMPLE HABITS OF
EXTRAORDINARY
SALESPEOPLE

Chapter 1
THE ASSIGNMENT 1

Chapter 2
HOW TO 13

Chapter 3
SIMPLE HABITS 1, 2, 3, 4.................... 25

Chapter 4
SIMPLE HABITS 5, 6, 7........................47

Note. In order to reinforce the reader's appreciation for these skills, *residential real estate* is used in examples to illustrate specific sales techniques. It has been the experience of this author that the guidance in the lessons shared apples to a wide range of needs/solutions, no matter the product or service.

Why residential real estate?

1. Most, if not all, of the readers will purchase or sell a home at some time during their life.

2. Residential real estate typifies the need/solution sales process.

3. It deals with selling both products and services.

Chapter 1

The Assignment

I received a call from the CEO of a large real estate company, asking me to prepare a presentation for his annual company "Kick Off" meeting on, "The Most Important Quality Needed to Become a Very Successful Salesperson."

Based on my experience, there is not just one "most important quality." Instead, there are several equally important qualities that are needed to become a very successful salesperson.

I knew the audience would be rich with highly compensated, successful salespeople and sales managers who were overly confident in their abilities. It was safe to assume the audience would prefer not to hear another presentation on "how to" when they already felt they knew "how to."

I was confident I could prepare the presentation the chairman had requested. The greater challenge was finding an opening comment or story that would illustrate *greater opportunity*. Otherwise, there would be little interest in sharing the experience and lessons I had learned on "how to."

The Ad

The following weekend, while reading the Sunday newspaper, a full-page ad provided an illustration that I believed demonstrated *greater opportunity*. A real estate office had placed the ad, which was designed to recognize the achievement of their salespeople for the previous year.

The ad was titled, *"Our Best Sellers."* The format resembled a pyramid, with a wide base occupied by the million-dollar honorees in very small photographs. As the pyramid rose, the performance categories grew, and the size of the photographs increased.

On the top of the pyramid was a large picture of their **Best Seller**, which announced the previous year's performance at "$25 million."

The *Our Best Sellers* ad recognized relative performance by adjusting the size of the Best Sellers' photographs and sales volumes. When annual performance was illustrated using a bar graph rather than employing photographs in varying sizes, the graph displayed relative performance in a more telling fashion.

Relative Performance Values

Each agent in the *Best Sellers* ad had access to the same inventory, the same mortgage rates, worked with the same management team, could attend the same sales meetings, enjoy benefits of the same education, employ the same business systems, approach the same real estate market, and so forth.

Yet, at the end of the year, the bar graph illustrated the result of their equal opportunity.

The relative performance of the "Best Seller" at $25 million was:

38 % more productive than the $16 million to $20 million club

78 % more productive than the $12 million to $16 million club

150 % more productive than the $8 million to $12 million club

316 % more productive than the $4 million to $8 million club

1,250 % more productive than the $2 million honorees

It is safe to assume, without exception, that not one salesperson in the *Our Best Sellers* ad began the year with the expressed goal of: "I hope I have a mediocre year."

One-Mile-Race Competition

If this bar graph illustrated the competitive results of a sporting event (for example, a one-mile race requiring four laps around the track that circles a typical high school football field), The Best Seller would have finished the entire four-lap, one-mile course before:

the $16 million to $20 million club had completed 2.7 laps,

the $12 million to $16 million group had completed 2.3 laps, the $8 million to $12 million team had completed 1.6 laps,

the $4 million to $8 million club had completed 0.96 lap,

the $2 million club runners had completed the first 137 yards of the 1-mile race.

At the end of the one-mile race, we could safely assume every competitor would surround the Best Runner and ask questions like, "What kind of shoes do you wear? What are your training habits? Do you have a special diet? How did you develop that kind of speed and endurance?"

Each year, I made a practice of congratulating not only the best salespeople under my charge, but I would call every Best Seller highlighted in local brokerage office ads to offer my congratulations.

These calls were more than just friendly adulations or flattery. I would then ask each top producer a question that might be similar to those questions asked of the hypothetical *Best Runner.*

"How many of your peers approached you at the end of the year and, other than offering congratulations, asked what you believe are the most important qualities that enabled you to achieve your incredible performance?"

The answer every time was that *not one peer* had approached these accomplished professionals to ask,

"What business practices guided and enabled you to achieve such incredible performance?"

That answer led me to conclude that the Best Sellers' peers assumed that the incredible achievement was accomplished by the Best Sellers' unique gifts of winning personality, wit, charm, and charisma. In other words, elements not easily transferred through education.

Strong interpersonal gifts are in fact, non-essential qualities. They often stunt a salesperson's growth as the salesperson relies on their blessed gifts of surface appeal rather than learning how to outperform the expectations of every client. In other words they see little reason to refine professional skills and choose to rely on charm versus professional development.

The best salespeople I've met are not the "natural born that way" types. They often lack winning personalities, charisma and charm. They tend to be: professionally polite, market savvy, focused, provide a valuable service and consistently outperform expectations.

The financial incentives to imitate the Best Seller are significant, yet few seek the guidance available by simply asking, "what priority guides your business ethic?"

Best Seller Ad Relative Earnings

Best Seller	$504,000.00
$18 Million Group Average	$378,000.00
$14 Million Group Average	$294,000.00
$10 Million Group Average	$205,000.00
$ 6 Million Group Average	$175,000.00
$ 2 Million Group Average	$ 50,000.00

The greater danger for most of us

Lies not in setting our goal
too high and missing it

But setting it to low
and achieving our mark

-Michelangelo

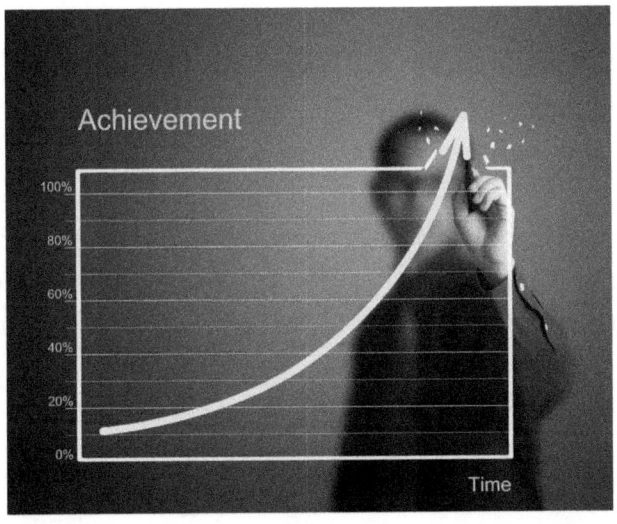

A meeting with the Best Seller's managing broker revealed that while the Best Seller had been a licensed real estate agent for only 7 years, he had achieved an average 50% compounding rate of growth over those 7 years. That's 50% per year—every year.

It was safe to assume that no matter how successful the salespeople and managers in the CEO's audience, it was unlikely that anyone could boast of a 50% compounding annual growth rate. Humbled by this stunning performance, I believed the greater opportunity illustration would gain their attention for the "How To" presentation.

The relative performance graphic shown in the Best Seller ad was not unique to the real estate company in the newspaper. The same annual relative performance is a common experience among sales organizations in every industry.

The obvious question is, *"Why do a select number of salespeople earn extraordinary incomes, while others with the same apparent ambition do not?"*

The answer. Extraordinary salespeople refine their business ethic embracing 7 Simple Habits designed to outperform expectations of *every client—every time.*

Chapter 2
How To

The fundamental problem has nothing to do with your behavior or your attitude.

It has everything to do with having the right map.

-Dr. Stephen R Covey

Every sales activity begins with *Opportunity* and ends in the *Quality of Result*. The Quality of Result is reliant on the *Quality of Experience* as it moves through 7 influencing elements (Habits). The better the experience—the better the result.

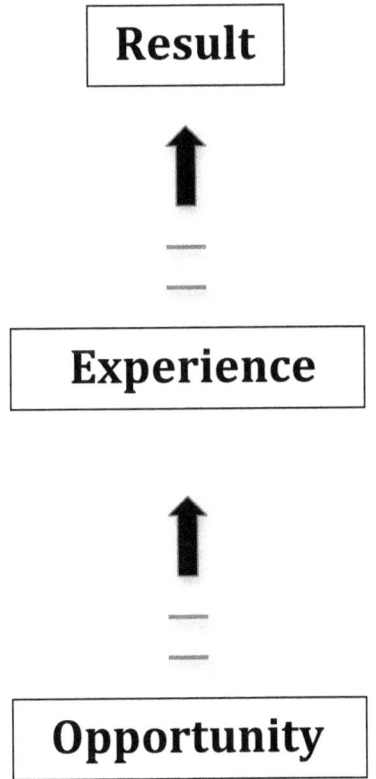

For example:

If a potential client felt their interaction with a salesperson was a bad experience, it would produce a bad result.

If a potential client felt their interaction with a salesperson was a fair experience it would produce a fair result.

If a potential client felt their interaction with a salesperson was a very good experience it would produce a very good result.

Extraordinary salespeople respect the 7 interactive influences (habits) that always affect the Quality of Result.

In order to fully appreciate the value of the 7 influencing elements, the salesperson should begin by reviewing each element in the Influence (Habit) Matrix. Once the review is complete, the salesperson is in position to rate the strength in each element as it relates to their business practices.

Picture a battery power meter attached to each element in order to measure the strength of each element as it applies to the salesperson's business practices.

Best results begin by identifying the salesperson's weakest habit in the Influence Matrix. As the salesperson improves their proficiency with their weakest influencing element, not only do they improve their performance with that element, they will also improve their total performance.

Strengthening the Weakest Link in the Chain Strengthens the Chain

Every profession has Skill Components. Take a sport like tennis for example. The skills might be: Preparation, Service, Forehand, Backhand, and Court Management. Many tennis players possess a strength they tend to rely on and ignore their weaker skills. E.g. *I have a wicked serve.*

It is unlikely their game will improve unless they allocate time focusing on skill development beginning with their weakest skill component. It is the weakest skill element that impedes growth.

Tennis Skills Components

Preparation	Serve	Backhand	Forehand	Court Management

If the backhand proves to be the weakest skill element, the tennis skill development map guides the player to focus on the fundamentals of the backhand—and only their backhand. As the player's backhand improves, so does their confidence and enthusiasm for the entire game.

Come on, hit it to my backhand side, I dare you!

Once the backhand is no longer the weakest skill, the player reviews the skill components and moves to the next skill component that is now the weakest skill element of their game.

Similar to the tennis example, the salesperson selects the weakest element in the Influence Matrix, which they believe represents their most challenging business practice. That element now becomes the focus of their development.

They should not abandon the rest of their game. They focus on the most challenging element one at a time. Improve an element, improve the total experience.

"If we always do what we've always done, we will always get what we've always got."
—Adam Urbanski

Influence Matrix

Result

7. Outperfrom Expectations

6. Need / Solution

5. Preparation

4. Tenacity

3. Ambition

2. Accountability

1. Integrity

Opportunity

Begin with the end in Mind.

—Dr. Stephen Covey

As an objective, Outperforming Expectations serves as that mindful goal, which strengthens every element in the Influence Matrix.

If you don't know where you are going, chances are you just might wind up someplace else.

—Yogi Berra

Chapter 3

Simple Habit
#1

Integrity

***"Whatsoever ye would that others should
do to you, do ye even so to them"***

—Preamble, "Code of Ethics and
Standards of Practice" N. A. R.

Integrity >> Accountability >> Ambition >> Tenacity

Integrity. If there is one influence that is often undervalued, it is Implicit Integrity. The market finds Implicit Integrity refreshing and irresistible. Demand has always exceeded supply.

Many people begin a career as a salesperson believing they possess a strong sense of Integrity, but the lure of a large immediate commission (and every commission is large) often causes the fabric of Integrity to fray. The lust of such a large incentive so close at hand can cause momentary distraction, which will challenge the best.

By definition, Integrity goes well beyond the word "honesty". It includes, but is not limited to: dependability; reliability; consistency of actions, values, methods, principles and ethical behavior.

The whole is equal to the sum of it's parts
—Aristotle

Honesty. Frequently a salesperson knows something the client demands feels a bit on the fuzzy side of right, but a potential commission can provoke self-justifying rationale in order to proceed with either what might be judged as inappropriate action or silence.

The profitable alternative is halting the conversation, with confidence that honesty is the best policy, and explaining that in order to serve their best interests you would like to consult with your broker.

On Guard. It's very important for salespeople to be on guard for leading questions or statements, which are tough to address as the honest response might develop in unpleasant confrontation.

Better to respond honestly at those times than carry the emotional scar that you might have been less than completely honest forever. Having the courage to respond honestly in uncomfortable moments leads to a powerful sense of professional confidence, which is a wonderful asset.

Anything less than bold honesty is never defendable— never.

It's been my experience that greed is trumped by integrity to a far greater number of potential clients than those who push salespeople to skate close to an ethical edge. Should a given potential client not prove to be so disposed—move on, find another who is worthy of your time.

Would referrals or repeat business from someone who tempts negative ethical behavior be of any value to a salesperson?

The important question the salesperson should ask is,

do I provide a valuable service? If the answer is YES, then choose only those potential clients that will appreciate that fact.

It's rare to find a potential client who does not have expectations that are greater than the market will bear, which begs an opportunity for any experienced salesperson to stand firm on facts and demonstrate their well-earned reputation built on honest guidance.

Documenting critical expectation and process essentials in writing via e-mail is a wise practice. Otherwise, the potential client is likely to place the blame on the salesperson for falling short of an expectation, as they may not remember where they developed an expectation that cannot be delivered.

When is dependability defined? Is the salesperson always on time or early for every appointment? Do they provide information and documents exactly as and when they say they will? Or do they offer excuses:

What the salesperson says: *"Sorry I am late, but my last appointment took longer than I expected,"* the prospect hears, *"You don't plan well, you're not organized—we must be a less important priority with you".*

Unfortunately, the current environment in business views being late as an acceptable practice.

A long habit of "not" thinking a thing is wrong gives it the superficial appearance of being right

—Thomas Paine

Small, seemingly insignificant breaches of Integrity opens questions with a potential client as to where the limits of breaching reliability and dependability may be with the salesperson.

Saying you're sorry for a breach might work once, but only once at best. After that, it belittles the offended and damages the reputation of the salesperson.

What you are speaks so loudly that I cannot hear what you say you are

—Ralph Waldo Emerson

The opportunity to acquire an exclusive listing is always a stimulating competitive experience.

It's not uncommon for a listing agent to hear a seller mention, "another agent I spoke with told me they where confident they could sell my house for $XXX,XXX". The other agent's $XXX,XXX happens to be an appropriate amount.

Knowing it's hard for a seller to resist the promise of a higher sales price, a weak salesperson might fear the listing opportunity will be lost unless they suggest that they can generate a higher selling price. What they should be prepared to do is, present the reasons why they are the best salesperson to employ for the task at hand, assuming the reasons exist. Always deal from strength—never weakness.

Suggesting an amount above market is normally referred to as trying to "buy the listing".

Buying a listing is bad business for 2 fundamental reasons:

1. Management Intensity. An above market listing seldom generates market interest. This will cause the seller to challenge the listing agent frequently, which can be cause for less than honest defensive replies. A relationship that began on a lie begs more lies.

    The constant challenge is disruptive, distracting and stressful. Time and money otherwise spent generating new business is taxed. It's a negative pattern of behavior, which breeds negative behavior.

2. Lost Business. It's hard to focus on new good business when the salesperson is burdened with old *bad* business issues. It's unlikely the overpriced listing will sell for the promised price, which will anger the seller.

The listing agents reputation is tarnished and the seller will hardly provide the all-important successful sales career elements of referrals and repeat business. That is an expense no salesperson can afford.

When a property owner decides to list their property for sale, they want to sell the property now—not 9 months or a year from now—but now. When a salesperson pursues a listing, they want to sell the listing now, not 9 months from now—but now.

The biggest waste of time and money is attempting to do something well that we shouldn't be doing at all

Sins of Omission. 25 years ago a residential real estate purchase agreement was typically no more than 4 pages, front-and-back. Today most residential real estate purchase agreements have increased by 300% or more (+12 pages) as they beg important disclosures, which in the past were the cause of painful lessons that could no longer unfairly hide behind *Buyer Beware*

If the salesperson is not prepared to explain the needed disclosures before the transaction executes, how can they possibly think they could explain the absence of a disclosure after the sale is closed?

Nothing provides greater confidence, extraordinary reputation, thundering growth and enthusiasm for the task than integrity.

The better the experience—the better the result.

I'll take the high road.
You can take any other road you want
And I'll earn 3 times the money you will
—*Charlie Johnson*

Simple Habit
#2

Accountability

*Every excuse I ever heard made perfect
sense to the person who made it.*

—Dr. Daniel T. Durbin

Integrity >> **Accountability** >> Ambition >> Tenacity

As a young salesman, I was upset while driving home from work late one evening. I had worked very hard on a proposal that had been rejected that afternoon. I blamed the client. Disappointment turned into anger as I drove. I told myself the lost sale was not my fault, but it was the stupid client's fault.

The radio was tuned to a popular drive time evening news channel. The sponsor of the popular news program, a large local financial institution, opened the program every evening with a short presentation by Earl Nightingale.

Mr. Nightingale had achieved considerable prominence as a speaker, business coach, author, and trainer. Mr. Nightingale's deep, wonderful, deep charismatic voice fortunately interrupted my anger.

His program that evening was called "The Magic Word." I don't recall every word of Mr. Nightingale's presentation, but his message hit me like a lightening bolt. Essentially, he said, "It's a shame: the sales that are lost, promotions missed, and marriages tolerated, but unhappy —all because people wait for the world to change toward them before they will change toward it."

"I would have made that sale if only the customer wasn't..."

"This would be a great job if only my boss wasn't so…"

"This would be a great relationship if only he or she didn't…" or "would…"

His message was powerful, and certainly appropriate for the moment at hand. I started to reflect on the sales I had lost and the disappointing outcome I had blamed on the client. I realized that, as long as I blamed potential clients for lost sales, it was unlikely my sales production would improve.

Mr. Nightingale's advice allowed me to realize that each disappointing experience in my life—be it professional or personal—was likely to continue producing the same disappointing results unless I attempted to understand how I might change my perspective—how I might react differently to produce a more positive experience.

Unless I was willing to change, the same disappointing events in my life would continue. The only person who can improve positive outcomes of any experience in our lives is "us".

The better the experience—the better the result.

To thine own self be true
—Shakespeare

Simple Habit
3
Ambition

Nobody can prevent you from
choosing to be exceptional

—Mark Sanborn

Integrity >> Accountability >> **Ambition** >>Tenacity

Dictionary.com defines *Ambition* as, "an earnest desire for some type of achievement or distinction, such as power, honor, fame, or wealth, and the willingness to strive for its attainment."

There was an article in a prominent national magazine several years ago that shocked my perception of ambition. This article, based on extensive research; stated that ambition is and always has been a very rare quality in mankind, no matter the geographic location, race, creed, culture, or gender.

I had always assumed otherwise. I thought everyone wanted to improve his or her lot in life. Not true.

I feel it's safe to assume you would not be reading this book or attending this seminar unless you were one of the very few who wanted to strive for achievement. You don't feel as if you were cut out to have a mediocre existence. You are one of those rare individuals.

Ambition has little value unless it is aimed at a worthy target—Outperforming Every Client's Expectations—every time.

Distraction.

I've been honored to work with some exceptional salespeople. I have witnessed many exceptional salespeople be exceptional for plus 15 years, only to lose focus and drift from the very principles that served them so well.

Some talented salespeople began to view an incredible income as confirmation of their greatness. Sadly, they often assume there is no longer reason to enhance and continue to build their reputation as a salesperson who always outperforms expectations. The result is a slow and tragic professional death.

Others, who enjoyed as much as 90% of their business from well-deserved referrals, began to feel they were doing their customers a favor. Sad, but all to often true.

The best way to avoid the destructive distraction is a maintaining business model that seeks to *outperform* every client's expectations.

The better the experience—the better the result.

What you get by achieving your goals
is not as important as
what you become
by achieving your goals
—Henry David Thoreau

Simple Habit
4

Tenacity

Perseverance is the secret of all triumphs
—Victor Hugo

Integrity >> Accountability >> Ambition_ >>**Tenacity**

I mentioned an article on the extremely rare quality of ambition in the world. The article went on to say there is one quality that is even harder to find among people, and that quality is tenacity.

In other words, a few have an earnest desire for some type of achievement or distinction (power, honor, fame, or wealth) and the willingness to strive for its attainment. They lack simple perseverance needed to maintain drive.

An often-heard adage is, "If at first you don't succeed, try, try again." Makes sense—sounds easy, but isn't.

The sharp knife of Tenacity dulls as it encounters disappointment, discouragement, periodic management intense workloads and distractions. Disappointment challenges perseverance. The journey starts to feel as if it were an uphill walk into the wind. I believe Michael Jordan might have said, "I am not afraid to fail. I am afraid I won't continue to try."

Growth processes are built on a lot of, "Whoops, that didn't happen as planned the first few times." Teaching someone to ride a bike includes teaching him or her the need for second effort. It is unlikely the first attempt will succeed. However, each subsequent effort advances skill development.

The same holds true for any worthy goal. Do not abandon the objective because the initial effort is not an easy success.

Success rewards continued effort in the face of, "Whoops, that didn't happen as planned the first few times." It's called tenacity. I have yet to meet a person who achieved significant accomplishment without employing the virtue of tenacity. Know it is a common practice for the many to quit when first efforts fail. Reach beyond the common experience that challenges so many.

The best defense against the inevitable challenges that discourage second effort is *anticipation*. Understand that the nature of business and life in general is, "the best plans will not always turn out as anticipated". Accept that fact and be prepared to ignore disappointment, discouragement, and the distraction that causes disappointing outcomes.

Few salespeople receive encouragement, praise, and positive motivation from an external source; "You are a very talented salesperson (or manager)." "You are a great friend." "I couldn't wish for a better husband or wife." The best salespeople recognize that is the nature of life and focus on *their* goal. They do not need external affirmations.

The great salespeople hold a powerful confidence of conviction in the face of disappointing outcomes. The only thing that matters to them is knowing they will achieve as long as they anticipate the need for continual effort.

The better the experience—the better the result.

I have missed more than 9,000 shots in my career. I have lost almost 300 games. On 26 occasions I have been entrusted to take the game-winning shot . . . and I missed

I have failed over and over and over again in my life. And that's precisely why I succeed

—Michael Jordan

Simple Habits
#1 through #4

The better the experience—the better the result.

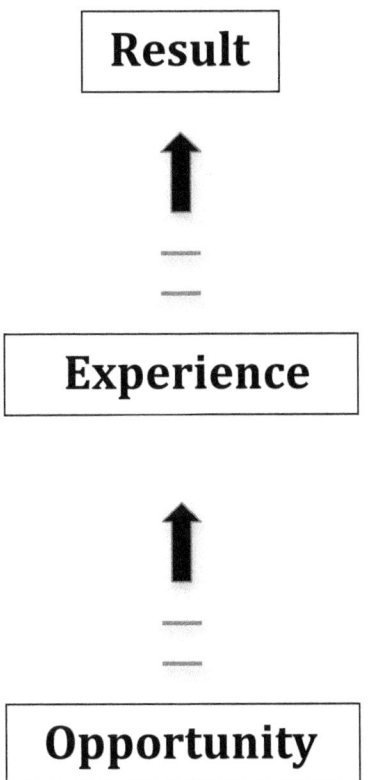

Chapter 4
Simple Habits 5, 6, 7

Preparation

Need/Solution

Outperform Expectations

Simple Habit
5
Preparation

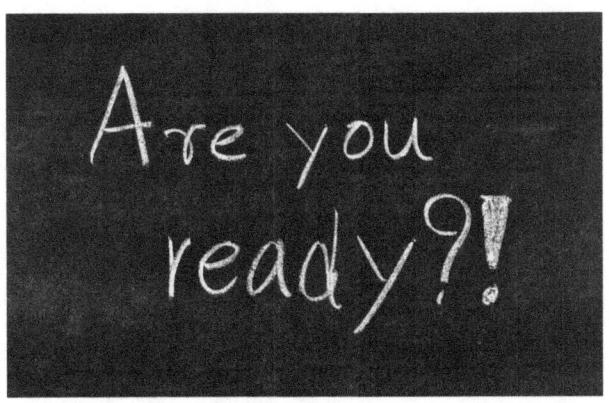

*To each there comes in their lifetime
a special moment when they are
figuratively tapped on the shoulder and
offered the chance to do a very special
thing unique to them and fitted to their
talents*

*What a tragedy if that moment finds
them unprepared or unqualified for that
which could have been*

—Sir Winston Churchill

Preparation > Need/Solution > Out Perform
Expections

There are many claims as to the essential elements
needed to become successful. Many are valid maxims.
But nothing trumps Preparation.

*Give me six hours to chop down a tree
and I will spend the first four
sharpening the axe*

—Abraham Lincoln

*It's not the will to win that matters
everyone has that. It's the will to prepare
to win that matters*

—Paul "Bear" Bryant

Simple Habit
5
Preparation

a) Organizational Skills

b) Punctuality.

d) Education

e) Practice

f) A Referral Marketing System

Organizational Skills

Becoming organized is not a one-time deal. It is a constant work in progress
—Charisse Ward

A common frustration I hear from many salespeople is. *"I need to become more organized. I've tried everything, but nothing seems to work."*

Organizational challenges often include lost keys, running behind schedule, misplaced files, scheduling conflicts, trade partners who are not performing as scheduled, interruptions and so forth.

Poor organizational skills mean lost sales, which surrenders a great deal of commissions otherwise earned. This in turn causes lost referrals, missed repeat business, unwarranted stress, and the deficiency paints a poor professional image.

Despite these obviously self-inflected wounds, those with poor organizational skills sometimes prefer to offer self-justifying excuses, rather than investing a small amount of time each week to develop a cure. It's simply a bad habit—a repeating negative pattern of behavior.

Good organizational skills are like a very good knife. Even the best knife needs to be constantly sharpened.

Good order is the foundation of all things
—Edmund Burke

Improving Organizational Skills

1. Schedule a regular (no variance, no excuses, no rescheduling) 30-minute "do-not-disturb" meeting with yourself each week titled "improving MY organizational skills."
2. List all of your organizational deficiencies in bold font on a Word document.
3. Think about solutions for each one.
4. Write potential solutions beneath each deficiency.
5. Spend the first 5 minutes each day reading your challenges and solutions.

6. Apply your solutions (to the best of your ability) over the next 7 days.

7. Repeat this process each week. Review the solutions that you believe should have worked, but perhaps need adjustment, or consider alternative methods. Add the refined solution below the previous solution. Do not erase the one above. Save it for weekly review.

8. Continue the practice each week. You will get rid of bad habits by replacing them with a good habit and positive patterns of behavior

This method is very effective. The process also sharpens ingenuity and initiative skills.

Do not cancel your weekly *My Organization Improvements Meeting*. Bad organizational habits are not genetic traits. They are simply a negative pattern of behavior—a bad habit. It is the result of trying to do too much, too fast, too often.

Over Scheduling Tip: *Learn how to say No!*

The better the experience—the better the result.

Good habits, once established, are just as hard to break as are bad habits

—Robert Puller

Punctuality

Method is the very hinge of business, and there is no method without punctuality

—Richard Cecil

Many, including this author, believe that being exactly on-time for an appointment is late. A client may arrive at the designated location 10 or 15 minutes early. As the scheduled time approaches, they'll start to look at their watch, wondering whether the salesperson is going to show up at the appointed time. Walking into the room or driving in the parking lot right on time is perceived as being late.

It takes time to get out of the car, grab your briefcase, remove the needed files, and so forth. In other words, if the salesperson *is not* set up for the meeting with their computer on, needed folders arranged, refreshments in the hands of the customer, all items needed now removed from the briefcase, they are not on time.

No matter what the salesperson says, it comes across as an excuse for being unorganized, not being dependable, and not showing respect for the client. When it happens, the salesperson's gibberish remarks sound weak and whiny.

Clients also have schedules. They consider their time to be as important as any salesperson's time. Why make the statement that your time is more important than theirs?

How do you feel when someone doesn't show up on time for an appointment with you? Why would you expect a potential client to feel differently?

View an appointment as if you were scheduled to get on a boat that was to depart the dock at exactly 10 a.m. At 9:59 a.m., the captain has ordered the crew to stand by to release the mooring lines and prepare to lift the loading ramp. He has started the engine, and he puts the boat in gear at exactly 10 a.m. Should you arrive exactly on time, you'd better be able to run fast and jump far.

Being 10 or 15 minutes early for an appointment is never lost time. It allows the salesperson to relax before the meeting, review the planned agenda, layout presentation folders, and present the appearance that they value the customer's time—they're prepared to show respect for the customers interest.

Nothing is gained by showing up exactly on time. Conversely, showing up early is always an advantage.

Given the choice of arriving early or late, why choose late?

The better the experience—the better the result.

> ***Better three hours too soon,***
> ***than one minute too late***
>
> —William Shakespeare

Education

One's mind, once expanded by a new idea, never regains its original dimensions

—Oliver Wendell Holmes

Education—a necessary evil, or the fertilizer of growth? Pre-licensing and post-licensing requirements in many professions are often viewed as a necessary evil.

One is essential in order to acquire a license to practice; the other is essential in order to maintain an active license. When they are viewed as necessary evils, the result is "a little bit of knowledge can be a dangerous thing."

It has been my experience that many of those born with gifted advantages would rather rely on those perceived gifts than investing time and effort developing best business practices.

It has also been my experience that those who continue throughout their career to invest time and effort weekly in coaching sessions (skill development) become the most successful salespeople.

In the words of Stephen Covey: *"In the short run you may be able to get by if you learn how to manipulate the man-made rules, to play the game . . . In most one-shot or short-lived human interactions . . . You can pick up quick, easy techniques that may work in short-term situations. But secondary traits alone have no permanent worth . . .*

"But what happens when we attempt to shortcut a natural process in our growth and development? If you are only an average tennis player but decide to play at a higher level in order to make a better impression, what will be the result? Would positive thinking alone enable you to compete effectively against a professional?

"Each of us tends to think we see things as they are, that we are objective. But this is not the case. We see the world, not as it is, but as we are—or, as we are conditioned to see it."

One of the best residential real estate agents I know has been in the business for approximately 10 years. He has averaged 27 days between listing and contract over those +10 years.

Yet, he always has and still does participate in two 1-hour telephone conference coaching sessions every week. He treats those scheduled coaching calls as if they were scheduled meetings with very important potential clients.

He makes +/- $500,000 a year because he invests 1 hour twice a week on the telephone coaching sessions. After the first year, a lot of what he hears is repetitious (always with refinements and shared experience), but he listens to, applies, refines, and practices the basics of the more typical client interaction over and over again.

2 hours a week: $500,000 a year. That's $5 million in 10 years.

The better the experience—the better the result.

> ### *The roots of education are bitter,*
> ### *but the fruit is sweet*
> —Aristotle

Practice.

Practice.

Level 1. Licensing, understanding the fundamentals of contracts, forms, how to use the tools provided by MLS, etc.

Level 2. Attend in-office training sessions to better understand the intent of language in forms and contracts—support for understanding the tools provided by MLS (should the salesperson work in the real estate industry)—the *do's* and *don't's*.

Level 3. Working with an experienced peer or sales manager on appropriate replies to typical client questions.

Level 4. Utilize low-intensity role-play. There are many talented sales coaches who offer weekly telephone calls or online coaching. Most, if not all, provide role-play material that you can listen to or read. It is a beneficial and important practice, but there is a need to graduate to the next level in order to enjoy far greater results.

Level 5. Full-Participation Interactive Role-Play. This is probably the most underrated and seldom-used advanced learning tool. It is, in my professional experience, the best training method for any salesperson in any industry, bar none.

Many agents will read interactive role-play examples. Many agents will listen to interactive role-play examples. Certainly helpful training, but not in the same league as full-participation role-play.

Full-participation role play occurs when a peer or sales manager plays the role of a customer and the salesperson plays the role of the salesperson. They role-play a variety of sales and listing interviews that reflect the frequent comments and questions potential customers typically express.

It is important to stay in role throughout the exercise. No, "I should said this or that's". There is seldom a smooth interaction when the salesperson is second-guessing their comments or answers.

Smooth interaction develops with practiced experience. There is everything to gain and only a little time to invest in order to be prepared when applying appropriate practiced comments and answers.

Level 6. Aggressive Full-Participation Interactive Role-Play. This level is sales training to the 6th power. It is the maker of Master Sales Professionals. No matter how successful a salesperson may be, engaging in Aggressive Full-Participation Interactive Role-Play shocks any previous perception of full talent and ability. This process will elevate skills to their absolute best.

Level 6 uses the same "most-frequent replies, questions, and challenges" that were used in level 3 4 and 5.

However, in a level 6 format, the coach (or person who takes the role of a potential client) exaggerates, intimidates, raises their voice in rude interruptions and attempts to challenge the salesperson's ability to maintain poise and respond calmly and in a concise professional manner. The goal is to maintain poise under fire. The coach may be wearing thick Groucho Marx black-rim glasses with a big fake nose, heavy eyebrows, and a mustache.

Or, he or she may be wearing an oversized red wig and ugly false teeth. The coach may scratch himself all over as if he has fleas; look around the room as if easily distracted while the salesperson introduces the presentation; fake a stutter; constantly interrupt; raise their voice in intimidating challenge and so forth.

It is not hard to find another agent who would like to play the role of an intimidating potential client. They've met lots of them. Try it often. You will be amazed at how much additional poise and confidence of conviction you develop under fire, in any circumstance.

Seems stupid—isn't.

We never know, no matter how long we've been in this business, who is going to walk through the door next, who is going to be on the other end of the next telephone call. Aggressive, fully interactive role-play prepares the salesperson for extreme personalities and behavior. Anything else becomes a piece of cake. Confidence is gained at a most affordable price.

With some experience participating in an aggressive exaggerated interactive role-play, the salesperson is prepared to handle the difficult and unexpected personalities.

It is a learning process that yields refined skill in advance, versus disappointing reflections after the fact.

If new recruits in the military practiced combat exercises using lethal ammunition (versus blank ammunition), the results would be disastrous. When we interact with a potential client, it's always live commission, so why not practice when it's not live commission?

The better the experience—the better the result.

I try not to dance better than anyone else.
I only try to dance better than myself
—Mikhall Baryshnikov

Referral Marketing

Business owners tell me every day that the way they generate the most new business is through referral marketing.

Yet, they don't seem to grasp the power of this statement. Few if any businesses harness the true power of referrals by making the receiving of systematic referrals a cornerstone of their marketing efforts

—John Jantsch, quoted in *The New York Times*

Referral marketing is a method of promoting the service a salesperson provides to new customers through referrals from the salesperson's family, friends and clients. Salespeople can stimulate referral activity using a simple business strategy called a Sphere of Influence (SOI) business model.

Generally, real estate salespeople launch their career using a limited Sphere of Influence model. A SOI model is built on a strategy of attracting business from the people you know and at it's best aggressively expands the SOI by nurturing existing and new relationships.

A book worthy of consideration on the "How To" of SOI is Jennifer Alan's "Selling with Soul".

Growth in Geometric Proportions. Managing a referral marketing system is like planting a seedling of a tree that begins life with a few branches. Each branch produces more branches, and those branches produce more branches, and those branches......... The leaves multiply in geometric proportions.

The better the experience—the better the result.

Simple Habit # 6

Need/Solution Process

The first step in exceeding your customer's expectations is to know those expectations.

—Roy H Williams

Salespeople are better served when they view a potential client as a need/solution opportunity. Determine the need then seek a solution that serves the client's interest. Unless a potential client believes the salesperson truly understands their need they will have little interest in listening to the salesperson's advice. If the salesperson does not listen to the client's expressed need, it is impossible to present a solution the client with perceive as worthy.

Potential client's don't care what the salesperson can do or has done until they are comfortable the salesperson begins and maintains the journey with an appreciation of their precise need. There are many different methods that achieve that end. Many of those methods take on the form of restating the need frequently in order to assure the potential client the salesperson has not lost sight of the client's priority.

It's never about the salesperson
It's always about the client

Typically customers develop expectations that are greater than the market will bear—unrealistic expectations. A fundamental element of any successful buying or selling process is establishing boundaries early that manage expectations.

The most successful salespeople I know adopt a scripted proactive process in order to guide the experience to the best result. Proactive salespeople introduce a buying or selling process with defined boundaries, which causes the potential client to respond in a more productive manner. That process guides and directs the interview in order to avoid digression. It defines and maintains a focus on the objective. The salesperson leads the process.

Reactive salespeople rely on blessed personal advantages like winning personality, charismatic good looks and charm. They test their surface appeal with potential clients, looking for advantages. Reactive salespeople often refer to their method as 'winning friendship', while the proactive salesperson's method is aimed at winning respect.

In order for Reactive selling to be highly affective it has to run on all cylinders all the time. Reliance on reactive selling means; no bad hair days, no I don't feel like charming anyone days, no I don't like this person interactions and so forth.

Proactive selling works all the time with everyone. It's the most productive form of process selling.

Selling expectations. I firmly believe that nothing damages the reputation of real estate salespeople than weak listing practices.

Consider the sellers plight—disappointing expectations, anxious anticipation, uncertainty and the unsettling fact that *few sellers ever feel the net proceeds they receive are fair.*

When a seller looks at the preliminary closing statement the first thing they look at is their net proceeds and the related charges and fees. The net proceed amount always seems less than they desire. They understand they cannot dispute the need to pay; mortgage balance, transfer taxes, pro rations, but that large commission seems daunting especially since it comes out of their pocket.

Discuss commission before the fact, and be prepared to provide honest rationale. If a salesperson can't make sense of the commission paid by the seller before the fact, it is unlikely they will be able to so after the fact.

If a seller does not feel the salesperson earned their commission, how can the salesperson expect to gain the rewards of referrals and repeat business?

Buying expectations. Why waste the salesperson or the shopper's time if the shopper is not qualified or prepared to act on their expressed desire and respond to the solutions the salesperson's efforts produce. A mortgage pre-approval letter is an advantage to both the buyer and the salesperson, as the seller's agent will beg the question in order to understand qualifications and readiness of a would-be buyer.

Relative Value. When developing priorities for a home search there are 3 value influences that best serve a buyer: Regional appeal, Neighborhood appeal, and House appeal.

Should a buyer select a home based on an attractive price per square foot, which are normally located on the outer edge of residential development (lower land cost) and later feel the neighborhood appeal falls short on merits like schools, parks, neighborhood shopping to name a few, the buyer begins to develop regrets and the initial perceived value of the home is diminished.

The same can be said should the buyer become unhappy with the regional appeal on merits like transportation, proximity to shopping, employment, health care to name a few which cause the buyer to develop regrets which will also diminish the initial perceived value of the home.

Think of the purchase process like an archer's target. The goal is not just striking the target but striking the small dot in the middle (the house). When an archer aims down range they first look for the outer ring in order to adjust their aim (the region) or the greater geography of the target. Next they seek the intermediate ring (the neighborhood) or the more specific geography in which the objective is to be found. Next they will focus on the small dot in the middle— the desired result.

When a real estate salesperson introduces this process the result is lasting gratitude. Conversely, when a buyer feels remorse after the fact, they never accept the blame—it's always the salesperson's fault.

Buyers want and need buying guidance and education.

The salesperson should advise the buyer: that their clients who are most satisfied with their purchase begin with a focus on regional appeal followed by neighborhood appeal and finally the appeal of the house.

Show me a neighborhood I love, and it's only a matter of time before I will find a house I love.

Be a need/solution consultant.

The better the experience—the better the result.

The Market Buys Solutions—Not Products or Services

Simple Habit #7

Outperform

Expectations

It is an immutable law in business that words are words, explanations are explanations, promises are promises but only performance is reality

—Harold Geneen

Preparation > Need/Solution > **<u>Out Perform Expections</u>**

Preparation

Communicate in Writing

Under Promise – Over Provide

Client for Life

The goal is not satisfied customers,
it's ecstatic customers.

—Tom Peters

Spectacular achievement is always preceded by spectacular preparation
—Robert H. Schuller

Preparation. The guiding skill objective as the salesperson pursues quality of result has been Outperforming Expectations in the interest of the best professional reputation, repeat business, and referrals. In order to achieve this end, exceptional preparation is essential. The principal of *Ready, Aim, Fire* stands absolute. Change the sequence—change the Result.

Communicate in writing. If something is important, then it's important enough to communicate effectively—in writing. The best salesperson always conspicuously copies supporting trade partners and their previously-agreed-upon timing of their delegated responsibilities.

Trade partners also get distracted. Regular status e-mail serves to remind trade partners of their commitments to serve the clients' interest and the best salesperson's expectations of timely performance.

Written communication helps the prospect understand the number of people who are attempting to support the solution by outlining responsibilities and showing support for action or follow up. Written communication keeps the boat on the course and helps manage expectations.

Scheduling. Be early for every appointment. Schedule the next events, and / or meetings prior to adjournment of the current meeting.

Under Promise – Over Provide. Solutions often hold many benefits. Focus on those that answer the client's expressed need and allow the secondary benefits to demonstrate after the sale—pleasant surprises.

I.E. The 3 principal advantages of this product are a)., b)., c). . Subtlety introduces the others later.

Client for Life. Extraordinary salespeople communicate a continuing commitment to their clients at a closing. The salesperson has delivered the product and the commission has been paid, but both parties benefit when the relationship is continued.

Nurturing the relationship after the sale as closed is a great business practice. Inform the client of your commitment to serve their needs and keep them informed on financial trends, current news, and related real estate issues—long after the sale has closed.

The client stays informed and the salesperson's reputation is enhanced, referrals are amplified and the likelihood of repeat business is all but assured.

Maintain communication in the form of industry trends and continue to serve the client's needs and interests as an adviser or facilitator. Encourage them to call you whenever they have a question on any issue related to the industry, no matter how small a question may be. Establish and nurture a continuing relationship and enjoy enthusiasm for the task gained to it's fullest.

Simple Habits 5, 6, 7

The better the experience—the better the result.

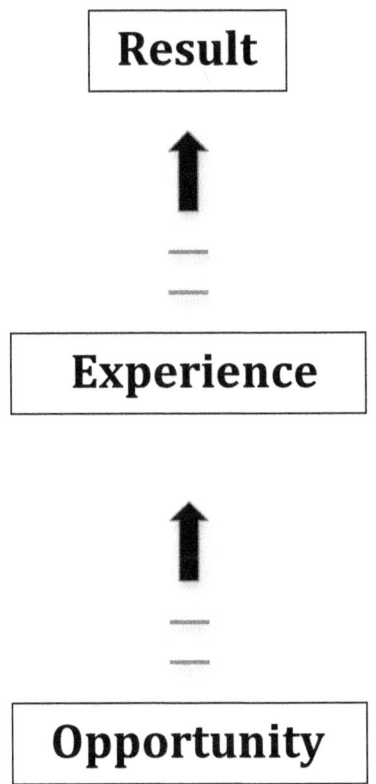

Result

Experience

Opportunity

*I saw the angle in the marble
and carved until
I set him free*

—Michelangelo

"THE LUMBERJACK"

A young man went west, seeking opportunity. Seeing a sign, "Lumberjacks Wanted," he applied for the job. The line boss informed him that his compensation was tied to the number of trees he cut down.

Blessed with physical attributes and attitude, ax in hand, he proved he was able to drop seven trees in one day, matching any of the "most experienced" lumberjacks in camp. He was excited by this newfound opportunity.

However, on the following day, he dropped only six trees. At the end of the next day he approached the foreman for advice, as his labors that day produced but four trees brought to the ground.

The foreman accompanied the lumberjack the following morning to observe. Sitting close by on a stump, the foreman watched as the lumberjack exhausted all effort to drop the tree.

Finally, the tree fell. Leaning over, hands on his knees and gasping for breath, the lumberjack asked the foreman if he had observed a deficiency in form.

The foreman nodded without speaking and stood erect. He reached in his hip pocket and pulled out a small, flat "whetting stone," which he tossed to the lumberjack.

Turning away, he shouted over his shoulder, "Sharpen your ax."

The Whetting Stone. Success is reliant on well-executed fundamentals. Appreciation for fundamentals often dulls or drifts over time. Daily scheduling challenges can be distracting. The experience interacting with the many potential clients can cause a drift—a distraction from the fundamentals of the trade.

A quick and easy sale can dull the well-founded value of fundamentals. It is an inevitable drift of priorities. No professional is immune to "drift".

It is not uncommon to leave a seminar or read a self–help book excited about some of the key issues addressed. However, those key issues often fade in a few weeks.

In the interest of short-, intermediate and long-term growth we publish a short monthly newsletter "The Whetting Stone".

The better the long-term experience—the better the long-term result.

Keep your ax sharp. It matters.

Go to:
www.michael2020.com

Sign up to receive the Whetting Stone and maintain a valuable focus on essential fundamentals.

Thank You. I appreciate the time so many readers have taken to write thoughtful reviews of this book. Your comments are helpful as I am always looking for a better way to guide versus instruct. In particular the many who feel while the title 7 Habits speaks to Extraordinary Salespeople the title could easily carry a substitution and apply to Extraordinary Manager and other vocations with minor refinement.

Recommended Reading

Alan, Jennifer
Selling with Soul

Carnegie, Dale
How to Win Friends and Influence People

Covey, Stephen
The 7 Habits of Highly Effective People

Drucker, Peter
Innovation and Entrepreneurship

Peters, Tom
Every PBS program, CD, and book presented by
Tom Peters

Walker, Al
The Sheep Thief

Notes:

Notes:

www.Michael2020.com

Notes:

Notes:

Notes:

Notes:

Notes:

www.ingramcontent.com/pod-product-compliance
Lightning Source LLC
Chambersburg PA
CBHW071341180526
45168CB00012B/661